FLOAT SMART

FLOAT SMART

An Inflatable Pontoon Boating Guide

T.E. Lewis

Schaumburg

Published in the United States by
eBooks2go and Gantec Publishing Solutions
1111 Plaza Drive, Suite 300, Schaumburg, IL 60173

ISBN:
Library of Congress Control Number: TXu 1-880-093

Contents

Three Principles

Stop and Ask Yourself Before Launching

Stop and ask yourself before launching you and your party into a streamflow (river):

Have I navigated this section of the river with someone knowledgeable beforehand?

Have I been trained to read the hazards of a river?

Do I have the ability to self-rescue?

Do I have the proper safety gear?

Do I know the proper hand signals of communication in case of emergency?

Do I have the peripheral equipment for my craft in case something fails or breaks?

Do I understand the International Scale of River Difficulty?

Introduction

T.E. Lewis plans, prepares, and peruses the elusive trout floating and fly fishing in Montana's outdoors. His interior river videos have been used by the United States Coast Guard Paddle and Boating Safety classes to help create awareness; he's a Swift Water Rescue Technician and volunteer for world renowned Montana Fish, Wildlife, & Parks. Lewis is the founder of Float Smart and the Float Smart Workshop designed to bring awareness to the exciting recreational activity of Class 1 inflatable pontoon boating for anglers or water recreationists who use one-person pontoon boats or are considering purchasing one. He's been a fly casting instructor, pro-staffer and featured outdoor blogger; Lewis's passion for the outdoors is reflected in his dedication to giving back and volunteering for national parks, national forests and state parks.

"Anyone wishing to float needs to carefully consider the risks involved and take steps to assure their own safety and that of other members of their party". - T.E. Lewis

CHAPTER ONE

Inflatable Pontoon Boats

Let me start by saying, choosing an inflatable pontoon boat is such a personal choice it reminds me of selecting your favorite fishing rod. Many times it's the experience we've had with the equipment which for me includes the quality of design and performance in-the-field. In choosing the proper inflatable pontoon boat you have to decide what your floating adventure objective will be, then begin to research and navigate through the hype. *The most important point I can share with you is to ask to see the owner's manual before purchase if possible*. Too many times I've had folks show up to share their new inflatable pontoon boat purchase and tell me they had been told it would handle any classification of water. Wrong!

Having recognized many of these different makes and models over the years I would have to inform the person that I don't think the salesperson told you correctly. Politely, I would suggest to the person if you open the box the boat is in, and retrieve the owner's manual you'll see the manufacturer rated the boat for Class 1 water. Startled by the knowledge that the boat is actually a Class I, it's usually back in the box and back to the store. The technical problem is navigating a Class 1 boat into a Class III or higher environment. – Not so good.

When possible, speak with others that may have the same model pontoon boat and research the reviews that have been given on that particular pontoon boat. Look for the boat's performance records and the manufacturer's warranty reputation. Do they stand behind their product? With inflatable pontoon boats a person generally deals with two different environments: moving water known as river current or streamflow and still water which is a lake or pond. I personally like a 9' to 10' inflatable pontoon boat for rivers with 7' oars which can easily cross over to be used on still water lakes and ponds. These are generally in the 70lb. to 80lb. weight range. In the past, fishing friends helped each other to the water. Now manufacturers are realizing the importance of a wheel attachment which works fantastically for one person to move boat and gear to the water. Lol, all those years of carrying and dragging pontoon boats and I mean who'd a thought... right? Considering the wheel has been serving the human species for a while now.

Smaller length inflatable pontoon boats generally come with 5' oars and are fine if you choose them to recreate on lakes and ponds. However, based on years of experience in the field, the longer and wider the boat the more stable. Longer oars allow for more bite in the water or power to navigate a river. Inflatable pontoon boat oars can be fixed known as clamp-on's or non-fixed which spins freely in the oar lock. Which one is best for you? Well, there seems to be a love-hate relationship with either option so you'll have to experiment to decide what's comfortable and safe for your floating adventures.

In the photo below is an example of a Clamp-on oar lock or fixed oar.

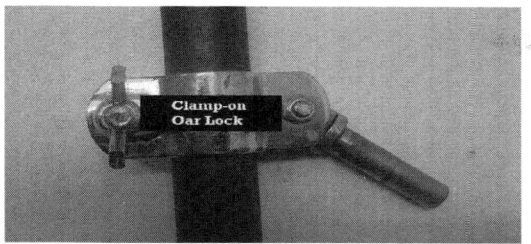

The above example is okay for lakes but has no cotter pin in the bottom insert (copper colored pointing southeast) shaft. If you're going to float rivers, make sure the pontoon boat you choose has that pin or it can bounce out on you even though the shafts are inserted into the frame and you're left trying to navigate with one oar on a river.

Non-fixed oars will be able to spin around in the oar locks. I've used both fixed and non-fixed but again this will be up to you and what you're comfortable using. The photo below shows an oar that can spin freely in the oar lock with the oar stop keeping it in place.

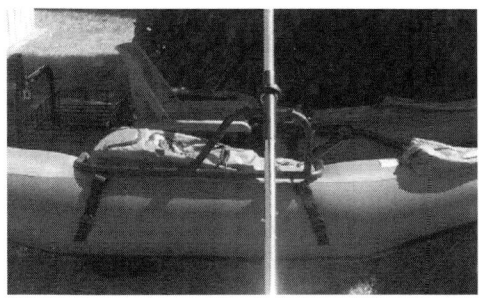

"Once you've purchased your inflatable pontoon boat take time to get acquainted with the boat, parts, and become familiar with the owner's manual including warnings."

My goodness, where are my manners? Here's a look at basic terminology to acquaint you with the inflatable pontoon boat and to help navigate this guide.

Pontoons

Pontoon frames including platform, rear cargo, and seat frame.

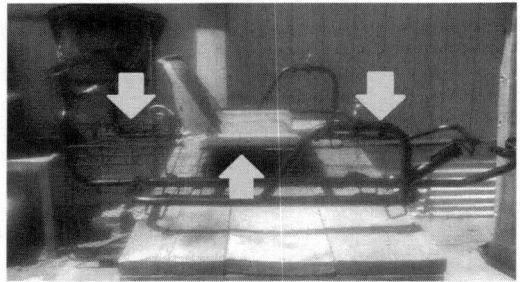

Foot Pegs

Oar lock & oar lock cotter pin

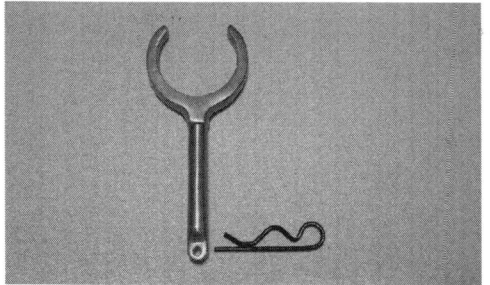

Clevis Pin

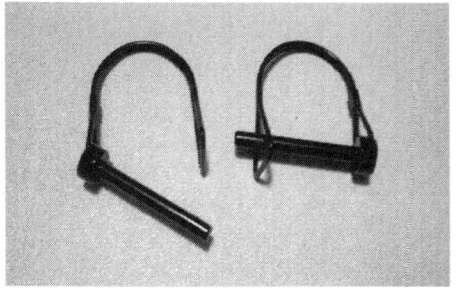

Pontoon Bladder

Pontoon Skins

Apron or Stripping Apron (fly fishing)

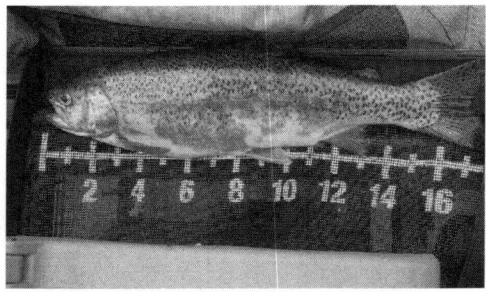

For safe inflatable pontoon boat management and navigation it is imperative for the angler or recreationalist to become familiar with the use of equipment.

Do you know your equipment well enough to enable you to negotiate safely around the potential hazards?

Once familiar with your pontoon boat, equipment, and owner's manual then the **first step** is take your inflatable pontoon boat to still water (lake or pond) and begin to learn how to navigate the craft correctly. Hint – Make sure to know the local boating laws before you launch.

Take time and get comfortable building your confidence with navigation and methods of using the oars to propel the pontoon boat. The power row is pulling the oars toward your body which means you're actually traveling backwards – To get a better perspective, research 'sculling'. The inflatable pontoon boat is a fishing machine and is one of the most versatile and transportable personal watercrafts a person can enjoy so this is an important step.

Enjoy becoming familiar with the inflatable pontoon boat. There's plenty of fishing action to be experienced in still-water environments.

Chapter Two

Know the Classifications

Floating adventures like all recreation takes research, training and building your technical skill. After you become familiar with your inflatable pontoon boat and are confident with maneuvering the craft the next step you might choose is floating rivers.

This is a different environment than still water lakes and ponds as rivers have current or streamflow. This current is constantly in motion and if a person stops rowing the river current is still transporting your inflatable pontoon boat and you.

Make sure to understand the Classification of your pontoon boat, sometimes referred to as a float boat, which the manufacturer has provided. The most popular pontoon boats are rated for Class I water. So what does this mean?

Simple. A Class I boat belongs in Class I water so when navigating down a river it's important to know that river's classification and the classification of the section of river you plan to run. Rivers and sections of rivers are classified by the technical difficulty required or associated with a particular river or section.

To gain a better understanding of river classifications look up and research the "International Scale of River Difficulty". Here's an internet link you can type into your browser to help you get started and become familiar with river classification:

Visit:
International Scale of River Difficulty
http://en.wikipedia.org/wiki/International_Scale_of_River_Difficulty

To conclude, this recreational activity requires an understanding of classifications from the inflatable pontoon boat manufacturer's recommendations and understanding the classification of the river or section of river you're floating adventure will be on. Oars up!

CHAPTER THREE

Identifying the Potential Hazards

So, you like floating adventures – well you're not alone. So much water – so little time. Maybe you're new to the sport or hobby – yes, no, maybe? How do you begin to research a body of water? How do you keep up with your favorite river, lake or stream?

Here is a list of ways:

1. Fly over.
2. Read books.
3. Videos or DVD's.
4. Talk to folks familiar with the river, lake, or stream.
5. Outfitter/Guide service.
6. Internet.
7. Physical Inspection.

"Awareness can impact lives & resources."

Remember, rivers are a different environment and need to be researched and well planned-out. Let's take a closer look at the potential hazards of floating adventures on rivers for Class I inflatable pontoon boating. Just because a river is rated Class I doesn't mean there won't be hazards and Class II or Class III challenges in your float adventure.

Knowing how to identify these obstacles or river environments allows the sportsman to enjoy a float & fish day on the water. Thinking back and reflecting about my personal float adventures, those trips allowed me to see some amazing scenery, wildlife and awesome fishing action.

Although called float & fish, for me it's actually been an **FSWPF experience or 'Float - Scout - Wade - Portage - Fish' adventures on rivers** and occasionally enjoying some swimming even though swimming was not necessarily part of my planned float adventure.

Let's take a closer look at the potential hazards that an inflatable pontoon boat operator can experience.

First for your consideration is to keep an open-mind about navigation and what could affect the decisions of a person operating the inflatable pontoon boat. I can stand four different experienced sportsmen/ sportswomen beside me - look at this photo - and we can all give you a different answer on what decision should be made to navigate this picture on a river. Interesting is that each of us would also be correct.

Factors like the time of the year, river current speed or streamflow, weather, and the height of the river make many of the differences. Important to the inflatable pontoon boat operator is to keep your eyes on the horizon as you float the river. Always look ahead, be on the look-out for the hazards that can present problems for you and cause injury or worse. Scout!

Second, distractions are the number one issue to battle while enjoying a float adventure. Let's face it - if you are angling and battling a big fish on the other end of the line it can be very distracting and cause a sportsman to take their eyes off what's ahead on the river.

Doesn't matter if you're fly fishing for trout or bait casting/spin casting for bass there's nothing like a good fighting fish that has your line stretched and your fishing pole bent while attempting to empty the spool of fishing line you have on the reel. It's why I'm there and it can be distracting causing me to take my eyes off the horizon or the up-and-coming potential hazards on the river.

"Battling a fish, navigating the inflatable pontoon boat and landing/ netting that fish takes some multitasking skill indeed and it's easy to make a mistake due to this distraction."

The decisions a sportsman / sportswoman makes on a float adventure will directly affect the outcome of the float adventure experience.

This is also why I recommend some type of certified formal river training so that an individual understands the language associated on the river. Now, you don't have to go through rigorous training and become an SRT – Swiftwater Rescue Technician but it's important to be able to communicate to others on a river. From terminology like river left or river right to knowing some of the basic hand communication signals. Rivers can be noisy and where a person thinks they may be heard, in actuality it's very difficult.

By knowing the proper hand signals you can communicate to others in an emergency situation your condition and a good river course will also help you to read river classification environments. The photo above is a great example coming up on a floating adventure.

You're floating in a Class 1 environment and the river splits into two paths - Do I go river left or do I go river right? And what are my potential hazards from these two decisions?

That big, obviously 'not going to move even during spring-run-off' object.

The river current has to go around an object like this whether it's big boulders like above or a bridge pylon. The no brainer is not to run into this object or its pillow on the upstream side which can deflect a pontoon boat. Let's look at the white arrow above and notice the river current division line or formally called an eddy line if you speak river terminology.

If an inflatable pontoon operator is not paying attention and crosses into this line the pontoon boat can be grabbed and turned unexpectedly. The second photo with two arrows that are connected shows that this eddy line continues past the object where we have the downstream current and the upstream current that is moving back behind the boulder. So the potential hazard to turn your inflatable pontoon boat carries past the object.

When it comes to rivers, the slower current is on the inside of the turn or curve.

Top Secret Angling Tactic -

Sportsman / sportswoman fishing? Now I can't speak for every geographic area on the planet, but in Montana, big trout not only hang-out in deep pools on rivers they also congregate in slower current located on the inside turns of these rivers.

When planning your float adventure, be aware that vehicles had been used in the past to help prevent soil erosion and they are still there.

Occasional after run-off you'll see them exposed, creating a potential hazard no matter what personal watercraft you enjoy. The photo is a shallow water example of a vehicle that got uprooted and carried downstream. Personally, I don't want to get tangled up with this chunk of metal while on a float adventure.

Once again the river presented me with a great shallow water example of this potential hazard. You'll recall my mentioning a person can become distracted while floating a river.

Whether that distraction is scenery, wildlife or battling a big fish, when on a river, you have to keep in mind you're in constant motion with the river current pushing you along. So when a distraction takes place for the inflatable pontoon sportsman we may forget to look ahead for potential problems.

"This shallow water example was easy to spot but let's take a closer look at a potential problem."

Suppose you're enjoying your favorite river float adventure and the fishing has been fantastic. You're navigating along then all of a sudden you come to an abrupt stop. Hopefully you have not been thrown out of the pontoon boat. Take a look at the blue line in this photo which represents water level.

You're enjoying your day and under the surface of the water lay this porcupine of a tree where you and the pontoon boat come to an abrupt halt. Pssssssss....sound begins or what is referred to as a 'rapid deflation' occurring in one of your pontoons and you and the pontoon boat are sinking.

You're on a floating adventure navigating a river so this is all taking place while the river current is still trying to push you downstream.

"I can think of many hypotheticals that can play out under these circumstances but will leave you to dwell on this potential hazardous scenario just under the surface."

Looking at the photo below, we see a tree with partial root base exposed and stationary at the time this was taken. You can't help but wonder what journey down the river this tree has been-on and what it experienced. Take an even closer look paying attention to all four arrows in this photo.

I hope you'll agree that we certainly don't want to run into the root base of this tree with river current pushing against us. The four arrows reveal a river current line or eddy line and if you're distracted it can grab your pontoon boat and turn it without warning.

Looking at the extreme right arrow you can tell that a pontoon boat would get turned into branches and limbs of the tree. Yes, it's very likely fish are holding at this structure which takes us back to becoming distracted. You could be concentrating on that perfect cast and BAM!

A monster trout takes your offering, then jerk, the pontoon boat turns and into the tree limbs and branches we go.

A good fisherman knows that structure holds fish and on a river that structure can also take hold of the inflatable pontoon boat and person navigating.

The inflatable pontoon boat is a fishing machine. It's versatile and transportable and has earned a reputation of being a very stable personal watercraft. The above photo takes a closer look at a tree structure that might be holding fish but this time it's in a still-water lake.

"I'll ease up to structure like this to pursue the elusive trout or aggressive bass any day on a lake but exercise caution and good navigation skills when on a river."

Every once in a while a sportsman finds himself / herself in that ultimate setting in the outdoors and with any luck is able to capture that moment. Here we see I've hooked, played and netted a trout while in the river that is pushing me downstream.

Finding myself in the middle of this river, eyes looking forward on the horizon for potential hazards, navigating, and battling this trout is quite the multi-tasking experience.

Take a closer look at this photo - What do you see?

This is a sweeper which is a potential hazard that hangs above water protruding from the river bank but low enough to create a problem for the inflatable pontoon sportsman. Had I become distracted battling this trout and not paid attention to what was up-and-coming on the river I would have been in real trouble not noticing this sweeper. What could have happened? Here's a few hypothetical's to consider:

1. Hit the sweeper, knocked-out and swept out of the pontoon boat floating in the river unconscious, pontoon boat and gear floating downstream.
2. Hit the sweeper and body impaled - pontoon boat & gear floating downstream.
3. Hit and swept out of the boat – conscious & wet – pontoon boat and gear- well you know.
4. Hit the sweeper – broken arm – swept out of the boat – attempting to swim – you know the rest of the downstream story.

I'll let you take it from here pondering on the numerous problems that could have occurred had I become distracted battling this trout and not navigated the inflatable pontoon boat correctly.

Dams – commonly overlooked but important are the operating information for a reservoir that influences your floating adventure. Many times water release schedules change due to weather conditions and power requirements. A sportsman should follow posted safety regulations and warnings including communications of releases and predicted elevations. Have you ever been on a river when a large amount of water was discharged?

"Pay attention to warning signs and marker buoys that are communicating to the public the potential hazards concerning dams."

In addition, danger buoys are placed upstream of some dams to identify a potentially hazardous area ahead and that access is restricted. Dams use horns, strobe lights, warning signs and spillway signs to warn the public and communicate impending changes in water conditions.

In high-flow the spillway at dams is used to regulate upstream reservoirs. Water is released through these spillways and below the dam can be turbulent and quite hazardous. Boats can be drawn from upstream toward the dam and towards the water plunging over the spillway.

"It is recommended not to anchor below a dam when floating."

Low-head Dams or Diversion Dams

From upstream, low-head dams are difficult to detect and don't look dangerous. Low-head dams can create a life-threatening situation and once pinned - escape is difficult.

It is a man-made structure built to divert or back-up water which is a backwash that traps and recirculates anything that floats - known to collect debris.

Boats and people have been caught in this backwash.

Strainers work to pull obstacles down underneath and out of the river current or streamflow. These are usually fallen trees or log jams which sit partially below the surface and above the surface.

Don't be confused. This potential hazard is not like the sweeper we talked about earlier which is above the surface of the water not in the water itself.

"Sweepers and strainers are very prominent on rivers."

Over-hanging trees with the root structure exposed give me the creeps. If it's safe I navigate the inflatable pontoon boat away from the river bank judging approximately where the tree can fall into the river. I personally don't want to be floating a river and have one of these fall in front of me creating an instant strainer. Timber!

I've been in the outdoors long enough to see trees fall and want no part of this while a river current is pushing me downstream and I'm trying to enjoy a float & fish adventure.

"On a lighter note, I also don't want a tree to come crashing down on top of me and my inflatable pontoon boat while I just happen to be navigating past."

Stoppers or swampers are a white capped wave curling back upstream. These are not what an inflatable pontoon sportsman wants to be navigating in for Class I inflatable pontoon boating.

These can flip inflatable pontoon boats and flipping adds to the list of potential hazards for the sportsman.

The frame, seat, and oars become a part of the hazard equation and can injure a person not to mention your equipment and gear are floating downstream. Flip a pontoon boat in a river, and you're fortunate enough not to have been injured or worse, you can still be stranded, looking for your pontoon boat, your favorite fishing rod, and tackle box etc...

Maybe your favorite camera is now tumbling downstream, hopefully not, but you get the idea. If you find yourself floating towards the scenario it is best to navigate the inflatable pontoon boat to the shoulder of the white capped stopper rather then running straight into this hazard.

Remember, we're talking about Class I inflatable pontoon boating not whitewater rafting. If I want to get into the whitewater I'll grab my whitewater gear, properly rated craft, and leave the fishing equipment at home.

The inflatable pontoon boat has earned a reputation of being a stable craft which is one of the reasons it's so popular, especially among fly fishing sportsman / sportswomen. However, did you know the inflatable pontoon boat when overtaken by a wave likes to dig into the wave itself? Remember, just because a river is rated Class I doesn't' mean you won't be running into Class II and Class III environments.

This is also why it's important for an individual to constantly be scouting ahead or looking out on the horizon to see what you are approaching. Concerning river navigation, maneuvering the inflatable pontoon boat into Class 1 water environments and portaging are tactics used consistently with inflatable pontoon boating.

"Let's take a look at some interior river examples concerning the subject."

Here I'm in choppy water conditions navigating through the waves in this section then out of nowhere comes this wall of water over the inflatable pontoon.

Here's a look at a splash down in another turbulent section of river.

Sometimes the wind can create turbulence in a section of river for the inflatable pontoon sportsman altering the conditions from nice and smooth to choppy even though I'm in a Class 1 environment.

Log Jams (strainer) – consider these extremely dangerous.

"While on a floating adventure I ran across this log jam (strainer) and according to the local news had already eaten a kayak and two rafts along with other floatation devices without oars."

I have recommended in the workshops I've taught in Montana for sportsmen and sportswomen to take a certified river training course to gain understanding of river terminology, to be able to read a river environment, and to understand the hand signals used to communicate in the noisy environments that rivers can present.

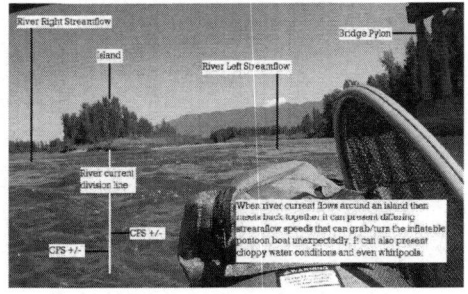

The above photo infographs a river environment while floating downstream with the inflatable pontoon boat turned backwards. The photo informs us, "When river current flows around an island then meets back together it can present differing streamflow speeds that can grab / turn the inflatable pontoon boat unexpectedly. It can also present choppy water conditions and even whirlpools".

A good certified river training course will expose a person to knowledge and verbiage used around river professionals. It's imperative to successfully navigate floating adventures and assisting in emergency situations should they arise.

Understanding the terminology associated with rivers like CFS – cubic feet per second, river right/river left, eddy, hydraulic, weir, portage, and gradient - just to name a few - are tools of understanding that every inflatable pontoon sportsman or sportswoman should have before floating a river.

The ability to read a river and interpret what's downstream on the horizon as you're navigating, is a cornerstone skill a person should develop. If you don't know what's ahead on a float adventure it's like not knowing what a stop sign is while driving. Even the most experienced inflatable pontoon operators scout and when not sure, portage is your friend when it comes to inflatable pontoon boating.

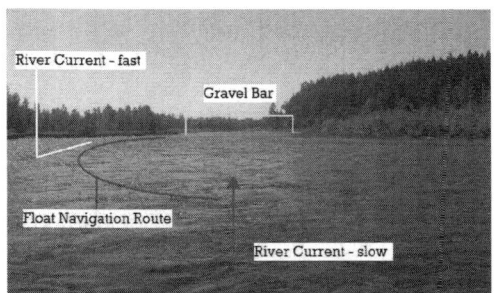

In the photo above you see a sand bar on the horizon. This sand bar stretches way across the river channeling streamflow to the left. If you have decided not to stop and visit the sand bar but rather navigate past, then the route above will begin to speed up.

The river current begins to speed up, transporting an inflatable pontoon operator to the left into the faster water. Be prepared for this increase in speed, as well as, hazards that may be between the sand bar tip and the opposite river bank.

Chapter Four

Are you Self-Rescue ready?

Are you self-rescue ready? Or How not to ruin your weekend recreation plans. After working hard all week the last thing I want is to have a weekend of recreation turn into a big disappointment or worse. Anticipating the unexpected, regular maintenance on equipment, and a good technical float plan have been key components for my enjoying float adventures.

In this section, I'll also be sharing broken equipment examples. There are many different ways to fix especially in the field. It is understood, we all have different backgrounds, training, and experiences on the water in various geographic areas and this section is a thought-provoking overview to create awareness concerning float adventures.

There are too many manufacturers, makes, and models to cover them all and the inflatable pontoon boat is a personal choice just like your favorite fishing rod, so keep an open-mind to get the best results.

I would like to direct your thinking to hiking in remote forest areas, the high alpine or backcountry wilderness areas. Most folks I know prepare for things like abrupt weather changes, emergencies, or spending the night in the forest due to some complication. Yet the biggest mistake year after year and season after season I've witnessed concerning floating adventures and inflatable pontoon boating is lack of preparation for the unexpected.

If you carry the extras hiking, why not on a floating adventure? Imagine you're on a float & fish and the oar lock breaks or the oar itself leaving you trying to navigate a river current with one oar. How about that weekend where you are doing a float and camp on a pristine lake and the oar breaks. Have you ever had this happen?

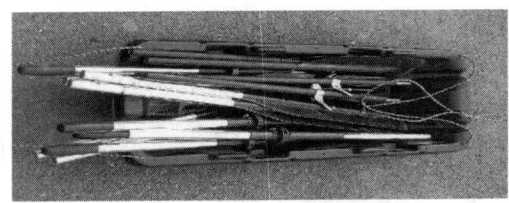

Your entire weekend is to row in circles due to lack of preparation, you're now disgusted and wind up bank fishing or just packing-up and going home. Worse is the fishing buddy not being prepared and he/she winds up bank fishing or turning into miserable company and just wants to go home.

I've had a fishing buddy bust an oar lock while on a float & camp and he would have been done for the weekend had I not carried the extra oar lock. He walks up to me with disappointment and disgust but I handed him an oar lock and a huge grin arrived to his face and the float & camp adventure was able to continue. My recreation time is important to me and I don't want it ruined due to a bad attitude from lack of preparation.

It used to be you had to make up a go-to bag of extra parts but inflatable pontoon boat manufacturers have become wise and are now selling kits that carry extra parts concerning their inflatable pontoon boats. You'll have to check with your chosen inflatable pontoon boat manufacturer if they offer a spare parts kit.

Let's take a closer look at "Are you self-rescue ready?

By looking at equipment maintenance, extra gear, and some broken equipment I hope to present a thought-provoking example why this question needs answering when planning a float adventure. *Base it on your chosen manufacturer.* Starting out here's a look at the inside cylinder of an oar with a broken rivet. Imagine floating a river and this rivet breaks. You lose the bottom half of the oar which connects the oar blade and you're now attempting to navigate with one oar.

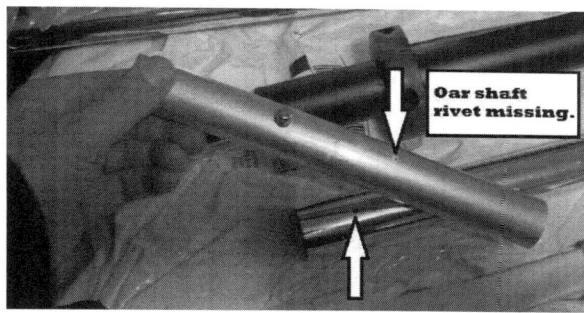

Ever have an oar stop slip on you? You've seen them used on radiators, water pumps, fuel lines etc... But have you seen a hose clamp used to secure the oar stop? Cost effective, easy to install - but not too tight - just snug enough or you'll damage the sleeve.

Oar lock busted resulting in the same as above; you're left maneuvering with one oar.

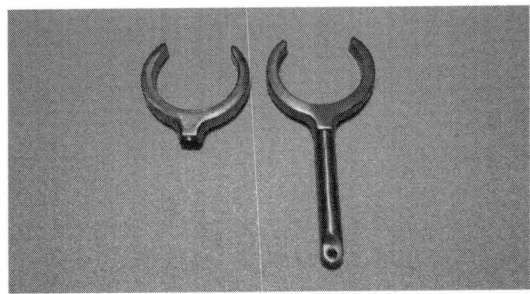

In addition to an oar lock I suggest carrying extra oar lock cotter pins. If one breaks, the oar and oar lock can bounce out of the bracket on the pontoon frame causing you to lose the oar and be in a one oar maneuvering scenario.

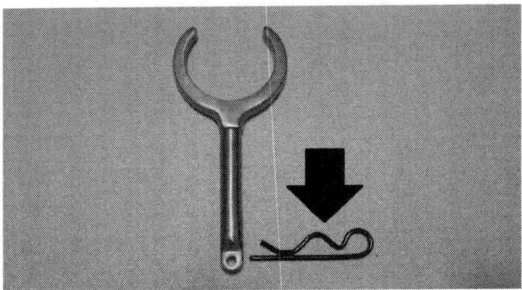

The bladder patch kit, just in case you spring a leak and your inflatable pontoon starts deflating.

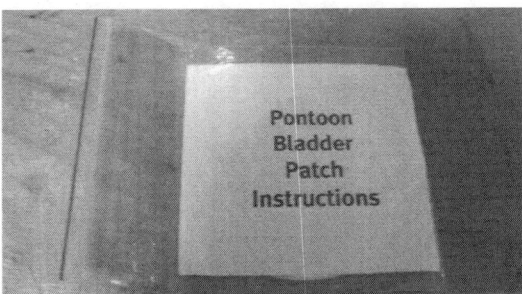

Are you Self-Rescue ready?

Carrying extra patches beats being stranded on an island in the middle of a river. I've patched enough bladders in my day and continued on enjoying my floating adventure. As I've gotten older and the storage areas of inflatable pontoon boats have become better I now carry an entire bladder with me. It makes for quick work to get back on the float.

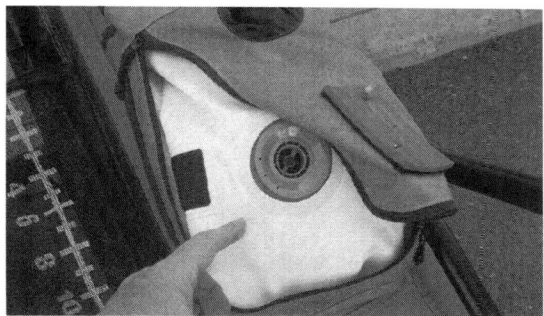

Frame clevis pins connect the frame, seat, and back cargo area of pontoon boats.

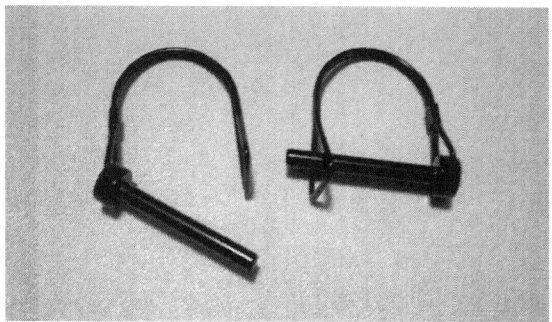

If frame clevis pins break on your floating adventure the frame can come apart which is an ugly experience whether on a river or in the middle of a lake. Frame clevis pins, like the frame, should be maintained and checked often for a sportsman's / sportswoman's safe floating adventures.

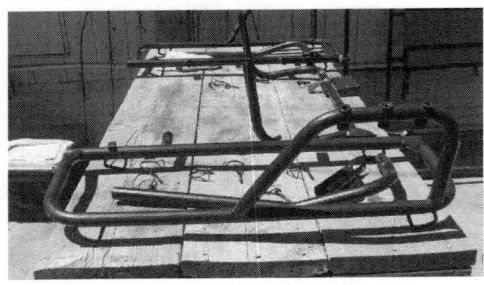

The frame clevis pin is also important to secure foot pegs on your inflatable pontoon boat. While on the subject of foot pegs, imagine if you will, you're in the middle of a float & fish adventure with the take-out ramp four hours away. You look down and your foot peg has developed a problem. With lots of water still ahead to get to the take-out ramp you discover the rubber coating is missing. What problems could this cause a person and how would you fix the foot peg?

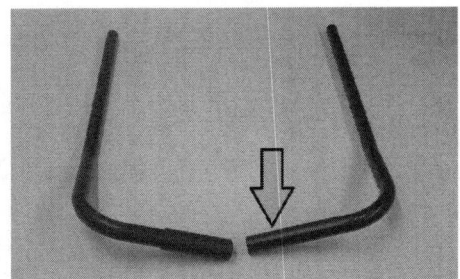

Are you Self-Rescue ready?

Your foot could slip off at an inopportune time, you could lose your balance, and fall out of the inflatable pontoon boat. Another scenario is a leg pin down against a rock which is quite dangerous if you're dealing with river current.

Have you thought about how you could fix this in the field? Here are some answers I've received from folks addressing fixing the foot peg problem in the field.

1) Duct Tape with surface of tape etched.

2) Safety grip tape/ black friction tape.

3) Skateboard/Longboard tape.

4) Velcro.

5) Wrap and tape medical gauze.

There are many ways to address overcoming this potential problem and it will depend on how an individual has planned their adventure.

It's a good idea to take an extra inflation valve and inflation valve wrench. Got a leak in your inflatable pontoon bladder and can't find it? Be sure the inflation valve assembly is fully seated for an airtight seal.

Use caution when working with the inflation valve in the field. A person doesn't want to over-tighten the valve or cross thread as they can strip out. Make sure the valve is clean and turns smoothly without any grit or dirt interfering with an airtight seal.

When it comes to float adventures on rivers and lakes, a pressure valve is a valuable asset for anglers or water recreationists who use one-person pontoon boats or are considering purchasing one.

Did you know that most inflatable pontoon manufacturers have a recommended P.S.I. for their inflatable pontoon bladders?

When you're enjoying a floating adventure on a river or lake many times the bladder is placed in an extreme temperature environment with cold water underneath and direct sunlight glaring down creating warm/hot temperatures on top of the pontoon. A sound float practice for the inflatable pontoon sportsman/sportswoman is to consistently monitor the P.S.I. of the inflatable pontoon boat while in use on a river or lake.

It's simple really. When you safely pull over and are taking a break check the P.S.I. of the bladder. Not only will it protect your investment but when kept properly inflated your inflatable pontoon boat will perform much better.

The absolute no-brainer is an inflatable pontoon hand pump. Whether you choose a double action that pushes air on the up and down stroke or not, these are a must for anyone floating and important for topping off the bladder P.S.I. during a float adventure.

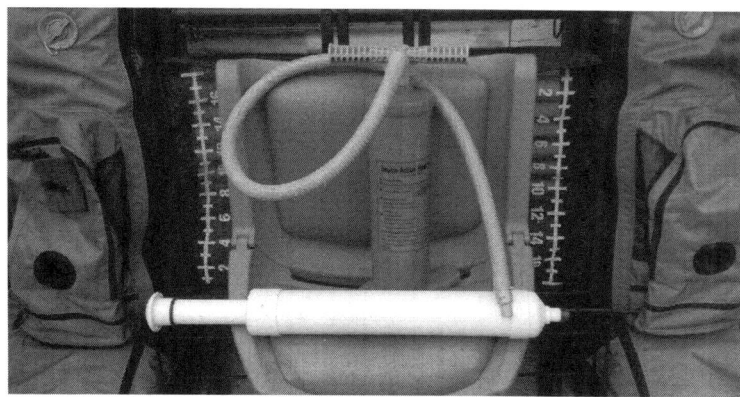

These examples could continue but I hope my in-the field examples have given you an understanding that float adventures don't always go as planned. At home and before launch a sportsman / sportswoman should design their exciting float adventure with the ability to answer this in-the-field question:

"Are you self-rescue ready?

CHAPTER FIVE

Gear Recommendations

Inflatable Pontoon Pressure Gauge

Inflatable Pontoon Pump

Pontoon Bladder Patch

PFD – Personal Floatation Device

Whistle

Water

First Aid Kit

Bug repellant, sunscreen, sun glasses, lip balm

Peripheral Gear Recommendations

(Base it on the manufacturer's design)

Frame Clevis Pins

Oar Lock

Cotter Pins

Inflation Valve

Inflation Valve Wrench

Wing Nuts etc...

Extra Gear Honorable Mention:

Oar

Dry Bag

Rescue Throw Bag

Helmet

"Awareness and preparation is essential to safe recreation for sportsmen & enthusiasts. In the end, it's up to the individual on how to approach recreation on water but keep in mind if you have to be rescued many lives and resources are at stake."

CHAPTER SIX

Waders? Inflatable Pontoon Boat?

Ranked at the top of frequently asked questions about float adventures are waders. This question was answered in a rapid deflation demonstration of the inflatable pontoon boat in Montana wearing chest waders with no wader safety belt.

Anyone who has been fishing wearing a pair of neoprene chest waders and accidently stepped off into deep water will tell you it wasn't a pleasant experience. To have water rushing in waders while attempting to hold on to your gear and get back to safety just isn't what was planned for a day's outing.

If a person chooses to wear waders and float in an inflatable pontoon boat it's important to know that this scenario could happen. In this water safety demonstration the description and term used is 'Heavy'. Water is heavy just ask anyone that hikes and carries water with them. Can you swim after the experience, yes but it is a struggle and I'm wearing a life jacket.

CHAPTER SEVEN

Visual Perception

I'm very comfortable in the outdoors enjoying the recreation activity of floating adventures. I can't explain it - It's just there. Preparation, planning, and then I launch the floating adventure to pursue the elusive trout. One of the thoughts I want to share is how I mentally approach floating adventures. What surrounds me? What are the dangers on the horizon or potential hazards?

Visual perception is the ability to interpret your surroundings in the outdoors.

In the photo above are we looking up at the sky or down at the water?

Here's another example of 'Visual Perception'. An important skill to develop is the ability to interpret your surroundings in the outdoors and especially navigating a river. The circles show winter conditions of an ice shelf or ice sheet that nature has presented. How would you interpret these circles?

Its early spring and the forest roads have opened allowing you to gain access to your favorite remote lake. Wait; if you're in terrain similar to the Rocky Mountains have you considered there's still avalanche danger?

CHAPTER EIGHT

Marking the Oars

One of the tactics I use when floating rivers is marking the oars on the inflatable pontoon boat. Watching for potential hazards downstream, battling a fish, or just taking in the scenery can be distracting and sometimes a quick and precise maneuver is needed to stay safe navigating a river.

I like oars to communicate to me the condition they are in while I'm on a floating adventure. Important is the oar blade positioning in relation to the water. Is my oar slicing?

Or is my oar biting?

The answer directly affects the inflatable pontoon boat operator's navigation and safety. Marking both fixed and non-fixed oars is a good tactic concerning floating rivers. The photo below shows a fixed oar or clamp-on which can slip on a person and then problems can arise while navigating.

Marking the Oars

Fixed or non-fixed, how you mark the oars is a personal choice but keep the marks close to your line of sight to communicate that something is not functioning correctly. When this happens a person navigates to shore safely and performs repairs, then you're back on your way. The alternative is that a person can lose their oar if not recognized in the early stages and wind up trying to navigate with one oar on a river. Have you considered marking the oar grips?

Here's an example using fluorescent paint on non-fixed oars.

Step 1 – secure and tape off the oars where you want the marks to be.

Step 2 – Apply the paint.

Step 3 – Allow to dry thoroughly.

The finished project should look similar to this example.

Marking the Oars

The marks on the oar grip communicate to me the orientation of the oar blades in relation to the water. Sitting in the inflatable pontoon seat these oar grip marks are in my line of sight or very close if I'm fishing and not holding the oar itself.

I've used everything from paint pens to emergency marking tape and this tactic has gotten me out of a jam or two being able to grab the oars and maneuver the craft with speed.

"Rivers are always pushing you downstream so they aren't very forgiving."

CHAPTER NINE

Transporting

I've always been entertained at the many different ways I've seen inflatable pontoon boats transported. From being triple stacked in the back of a pickup bed or hauled on a trailer they certainly have earned the reputation of being very transportable. Just remember to let air out of the bladder if transporting due to sun, weather and even a mountain pass which can all cause problems for you.

Here's a look at two different transportation methods I've used and believe me there are many but you'll get the idea.

The first deals with a long haul of two inflatable pontoon boats where two pontoon frames are secured on the top of the vehicle then the pontoons (skins/bladders) are carried inside an SUV to protect them along with other gear that is going on the trip.

The second is a short haul of two pontoon boats where one pontoon frame is secured on top while the second is secured to a cargo-carrier assembled and ready to launch with a little air in the bladders.

CHAPTER TEN

Action & Adventure

The inflatable pontoon boat has opened up an unbelievable world of excitement, action, and reward over the years in the high alpine, sub alpine, and valley floor. Like any hobby it takes practice, training, and research to enjoy this recreation activity to its fullest.

Rainbow Trout

Arctic Grayling

....to name a few fish species

Remote Lakes

High-Alpine Lakes

Meeting other sportsmen and enthusiasts in the field.

Travel

Rivers

and family or should I say the privilege I was given to begin training my son in a controlled environment to introduce him to this exciting recreational activity.

CONCLUSION

In closing, this awareness concept began from a float trip years ago where I reached my destination only to meet a family where the wife and child had to be rescued off an island inside the Flathead River located in Northwest Montana, U.S.A. Knowing that the couple had been floating this big river, each in a one man inflatable pontoon boat with children in the back cargo area sparked my concern for the safety of those enjoying floating adventures on rivers. Lack of preparation and lack of knowledge can quickly translate into tragedy. It was one of those defining moments and made me want to do something to help others to more safely enjoy this outdoor recreation activity that has brought me so much excitement.

It made such an impact on me that I altered my personal recreation plans, spent years filming the interior of rivers and lakes and finally planned instruction of a workshop tailored to inflatable pontoon boat use and safety that has been taught across the state of Montana.

I've been asked numerous times how this awareness message could be taken to other sportsmen and recreationists on a wider scale. Therefore I assembled this book - which can be referred to again and again with each season as a refresher and if you're new to inflatable pontoon boating may I be the first to say,

Welcome, to this exciting recreation activity of floating rivers, lakes, and streams!

"Just because a river is rated Class 1 doesn't mean it won't present Class II or Class III sections that the sportsman and recreationist has to make decisions to navigate successfully."

Recommended Internet Sites

A list of web sites to assist in gaining knowledge and insight concerning float adventures for your review. It's my recommendation to take a certified course about rivers to gain insight, knowledge, and to help develop an individual's skill level.

International Scale of River Difficulty

http://en.wikipedia.org/wiki/International_Scale_of_River_Difficulty

USGS – U.S. Geological Survey

www.usgs.gov

1) Science In Your Backyard
2) Real-Time Water Data
3) Daily Streamflow Conditions

Montana Fish, Wildlife & Parks

http://fwp.mt.gov/

1) Search: Cold Water Immersion

Float Smart

A dynamic, thought-provoking introduction and overview of inflatable pontoon boat navigation, peripheral equipment and safety.

www.floatsmart.info

Gear Recommendations
Inflatable Pontoon Pressure Gauge
Inflatable Pontoon Pump
Pontoon Bladder Patch
PFD – Personal Floatation Device
Whistle
Water
First Aid Kit
Bug repellant, sunscreen, sun glasses, lip balm

Peripheral Gear Recommendations
(Base it on the manufacturer's design)
Frame Clevis Pins
Oar Lock
Cotter Pins
Inflation Valve
Inflation Valve Wrench
Wing Nuts etc...

Extra Gear Honorable Mention:
Oar
Dry Bag
Rescue Throw Bag
Helmet

<u>Notes</u>

Notes

Notes

Notes

"In the end, it's up to the individual on how to approach recreation on water but keep in mind if you have to be rescued many lives and resources are at stake."

Made in the USA
Middletown, DE
22 August 2015